Clangings

For Christina —
With deep love for your
work and for you.
My Joycean colleague ...

Yrs,
Stan
1/8/13

ALSO BY STEVEN CRAMER

Goodbye to the Orchard (2004)
Dialogue for the Left and Right Hand (1997)
The World Book (1992)
The Eye that Desires to Look Upward (1987)

Clangings

Poems

Steven Cramer

Sarabande Books
LOUISVILLE, KENTUCKY

© 2012 by Steven Cramer

FIRST EDITION

All rights reserved.

No part of this book may be reproduced without written permission of the publisher.
Please direct inquiries to:

Managing Editor
Sarabande Books, Inc.
2234 Dundee Road, Suite 200
Louisville, KY 40205

Library of Congress Cataloging-in-Publication Data

Cramer, Steven, 1953–
 Clangings : poems / Steven Cramer.
  p. cm.
 Includes bibliographical references and index.
 ISBN 978-1-936747-46-7 (pbk. : alk. paper)
 I. Title.
 PS3553.R2676C53 2012
 811'.54—dc23

                    2012011890

Cover Image: Johann Fournier, "Schizophrenia" (2002). www.ether-elegia.com

Cover and text design by Kirkby Gann Tittle.
Manufactured in Canada.
This book is printed on acid-free paper.

Sarabande Books is a nonprofit literary organization.

This project is supported in part by an award from the National
Endowment for the Arts.

The Kentucky Arts Council, the state arts agency, supports Sarabande
Books with state tax dollars and federal funding from the National
Endowment for the Arts.

For my teachers

CONTENTS

~

ACKNOWLEDGMENTS

Thanks to the editors of the following magazines in which some of these poems, or earlier version of them, first appeared:

Crazyhorse: "My notion of heaven? Um, plumb garden"; "Okay, here's what we did. Dad was a quark"

Denver Quarterly: "A page writes me (my words blue . . ."

Field: "I hear the dinner plates gossip"; "Dickey's death feels all over me"

The Journal: "My tongue-print's on your butter"; "Nobody's safe inside the airtight zones"; "When I saw her, her face was a marinade"

Little Star: "*From the time he opened his mouth his talk was off*"; "Parents are the nations that thrust you"

Memorious: "Back on my wings, wings became me"; "First I denied the no-seeums speckling"; "I hear, in my phone, vocabulary where"

Perihelion: "At times I feel so much, I think"

Salamander: "Black cats ring bells. I'm your son"; "I'm speaking with my mother's voice"

Slate: "The circulars blued under my eyes"; "A finch in my chest flinches to get"; "Iris of the one-eyed Satan—see it?"

Sugar House Review: "Dear eyes, my ears keep paired for you"; "I cut back on coffee. And air. And sky"; "In your sleep they rant what's left of you"; "I shake my head, my right brain's"; "I was twin pencils. A fit in one sex"; "Mother said you count your friends on one hand"; "So I left my apartment, got down where"; "Tsk tsk, go my wits, like a grandfather"

The line, "pennies aren't worth much, but aren't worthless," is adapted from Cate Marvin's poem, "Lines for a Mentor."

Lines 3 and 4 of "Don't have to swim straight, dark says" echo two well-known passages from John Berryman and Robert Lowell.

Thanks to Lesley University for a fall 2010 sabbatical that gave me much-needed time and focus.

Thanks to Teresa Cader and Joyce Peseroff, who read me with more care than I read myself. I owe an enormous debt to Joan Houlihan, who helped me see the figure in the carpet.

Some passages in these poems were inspired by anonymous examples from the clinical literature on clang association.

"It is impossible to say just what I mean."

—Prufrock

I hear the dinner plates gossip
Mom collected to a hundred.
My friends say get on board,
but I'm *not* bored. Dad's a nap

lying by the fire. That's why
when radios broadcast news,
news broadcast from radios
gives air to my kinship, Dickey,

who says he'd go dead if ever
I discovered him to them.
I took care, then, the last time
bedrooms banged, to tape over

the outlets, swipe the prints
off DVDs, weep up the tea
stains where once was coffee.
Not one seep from him since.

What, you wander, do I mean?
Except for slinging my songs
wayward home, how do things
in people go? is what I mean.

A page writes me (my words blue,
made in a plant called England).
In school, England was London.
I blew World Geo. He was also

a tutor who purpled my crying.
I diss-cussed his eyes into a gray
blind man, being led by the boy
who spotted the viper winking

but won't say. It gets dreadful,
this hearing, only to overhear
bustling about me (over there)
whispers not not there at all.

Teach me a letter, give me a pass.
I need to work on my main idea—
the black eyes learn, a semi-coma
torn from a page of his masterclass.

Of all my inmates (okay, patients),
one mate I liked like I like myself.
Trained me to play dumb, play deaf
to the weirds. Called it patience.

Stashed my secret name in its haven.
Think I mean dick when I say Dickey?—
I do and I don't; or did, but won't say
anyway. Makes a greener chameleon.

And his name doesn't stain forms.
Stays taut in the face of taunts, refrains
from songs. Words *can* break bones,
but my silent one doesn't form stains.

Dickey hurled a foot through my door
is all, slipped fine out the birth-slime.
Someone's personality christened him
not mine. If floor lamps upset a floor,

his phrases bite moons into the dark.
I recover them behind my horn-rims.
Gored in half or not, totalitarianism's
tell-liar-isms won't make him the Dick

Who Talked. Quiet as a virus, everyone
lying inert he inserts into, stands alert,
becomes a member. That's his cavort.
I know. Holed in his yowl. Not alone.

If I think in yellow, I can remember
running with the blue-sprained boys.
And turquoise girls ruined my eyes.
I made bloodless my primary color.

Dickey says we're born in a reek
kind of ammonia, sort of a Comet
paste thickened with piss. The wet
crimps your nose and stinks if we kick.

Dickey's breath feels all over me.
He swivels the doors in their jambs,
pins my fingers till the pang numbs.
If he's not what I touch, smell and see,

with my feet on your floor, your feet
on your floor, why do I hear footsteps
in the hallway? Boot heels drum taps.
Can you feel him talking with my feet?

If I taste your vinegar, he's my thirst.
If I'm ground down, my window pane
magic-taped, masked, he's the Hurricane
on the tongue. Ocean's? Earth's?

My notion of heaven? Um, plumb garden,
symmetrically, what wanting rings about.
By the fifth or eleventh prayer—right?—
it'll come to some soul of an equation,

the aqueous solution at the equinox.
Dickey tells me it's a very big number,
a numb digit; particulate, therefore
it ducks the riddle grain put to the fox.

Forks can't solve it any more than a kettle.
Forks and kettles are found in the gospel
where they go horn to horn with the devil.
Look, here's his hide, bristling in a bottle.

How come certain hydras upset me?
How many earthworms fit in a home?
When did the cool of a garden go warm?
I think it stems from how He made a body

out of fish He couldn't school to swim.
Like a surgeon, with His slice to inside,
He overshadows the light he divided.
He created swine to swindle them.

The circulars blued under my eyes
from lugging salt sacks across a river
over a fire. One blinkered the other.
Almighty, they blazed with furies.

They were a sight. In Lord School,
my retinas uprooted. Not funny, I
tell you, spotting clots in eye jelly.
I've seen things. Threaded red pencil

threats, delivered. The pupils shrank.
Bobbing in floaters, I squinted right
at the nuns, white as off-white paint.
Faces have fifty-two muscles to spank.

Could've sworn I'd rubbed out all
that rubble. Could've sworn I saw
trouble swell into an eyeful of awe.
Awl, hack, rip, jig. Two-hand radial

Father Joseph. Touchy amen man.
Ass-burned the children out of sight.
Jesus's analgesics didn't conceal shit.
A hymn is one crummy physician.

It's not that I don't believe in God.
I am. My bible's on your bed table,
your prayer's in my prayer mill.
I was what I saw, which was good;

until what I was (I saw) was one
livelong hell, a still-born infant,
gene with germs. A germy bullet,
belief—believe you me. Take my son

alrightying from a suitcase airheads
hide their idols in, Padre. Parades?
I like parades—even ready-mades.
And he stirred a mass of fatty acids;

and four-and-twenty rainbow sets
boiled wax on twenty-four candlesticks;
and his foyer flourished with trumpets;
from the Void grew farm implements

until crypts shall hurl up apocalypse . . .
Likewise, it's not that I don't pray
(good way, by the way, to fire pity).
But man? O man. Still in the pits.

Tsk tsk, go my wits, like a grandfather
clock's nano-manacles. Shackle-tight,
I've read enough to know what a twit
wisdom is: makes the wild inside nature

mere recreation. An inexact psalm,
my chain of althoughs grows wider
and weirder, wired equiliteral ladder.
Plenty of Plutos left in the solar system—

true enough. From where I belong,
I rant, I stand, I decree: bears bite
if they're baited, lashed left and right,
toward the torches. So goes my song—

damn!—on the fritz. Obituary magi,
my top spins round with monikers
like Mary, Magda. So many Monicas . . .
Screw me on a cross, I can't tell why

I weigh so down when I get this mad—
tons of mustard seed times thousands.
Man, God's mistake; or God, Man's,
please deal me my get-out-of-hell card.

Sweat no longer creeps me out.
Sprinting up down stair by stair,
an inner barometer spins as I steer.
I feel good weeping through my shirt.

There's no point pondering what
brews in patios and pools. Nerves.
A stoic gets served the silt he deserves.
Don't let them see you sweat. I hate

that saw. How it panders to pain-
driven downpours, white migraines
blundering into a head's high beams.
Just let me blot the smudge my shame

sustained, sootier even than the psalms.
Thimbles of cool dew, my hand's heat
beading a punchbowl. On prom night,
the girls spited at my clammy palms,

gaggled with their lantern-lit dunces.
I treaded them dead on my trounce mill,
rung them on the risers of my elliptical.
Take this verb of spittle, you dances.

I feel as male as I feel female.
Dickey grins. No way he's telling.
He'll never spare me his helping
or fail to lick me to my tough and tall.

With Dickey I obliterate appetite.
We altogether decorate our wastes.
Best belted. Bells test our protests,
and we refuse to eat grizzly meat

if it's rare. Our flesh is his hers.
If we split, we'd mean fingernails.
The hammers that nail boys nail girls—
given to prigs as to prone ministers.

We made our cufflinks from handcuffs.
All our blotters need to soak up blues,
arm in arm, are Sparseland avenues,
dancers in our zippers, joints in our coifs.

Have us wear boas. Make us spawn
hamlet fish. Arrange us to clutch a
Ken or G.I. Barbie. Still gonna betcha
can't fork our brains, a tine at a time.

My tongue-print's on your butter,
come and enforce me, don't ask—
moist me, steep me, in your musk.
No wonder's turned you bitter.

Don't go all moot and crusady;
twitter your flute inside my sleep.
Don't bundle my pussycat in burlap.
Undo its tie, my aria goes screechy.

I hear (in my left ear, I swear)
a lobe stub its toe on your puzzle.
I can't stand you won't stand still.
If not me, who's this whole hell for?

Back in our ragtime times, jism
pasted pearls atop a bottom sheet.
The percale got pretty percolate.
Now it's sackcloth time all the time—

unless, unleashed, you hound me,
Dickey. Release. Furnace. Even
be feline. Fillet of my heart, quicken,
embroil or, anyway, boil me, honey.

Flirting from pokeweed, Dickey
flaunted his boy-girl bifocal look.
That did it. We took it to the dark.
Two takes two, unless one's a sissy.

We got married, not to get married,
but a house is not a nest it's grass.
After all, pokeweed poisons houses.
We vowed okay. Kissed, partied,

and got Sonny. Well, colored him in.
Planed and papered him, his people
parts stitched from patches, stapled
and . . . oh, play the rest on a violin—

moved downstairs, screened porch,
snoozed all noon; at tea, fed squirrels.
One proper cutie sniffed our peduncles
if we propped the door open an inch.

Then: sunset. She chomps the door
off, addles in, nibbles Sonny away.
Just like that: our pretty pretty baby
aborted from his green bell pepper.

I cut back on coffee. And air. And sky
if the sky started crying into seawater.
Because my throat clove to hunger,
and starvlings flew speedily in me,

for food I'd dish out grubs from trees.
Man, he growled, my Dickey. On axes
from Anarchic to zones of Chaotic, his
bile grumbled inside our twin bellies.

If an elf owl's about to kill, he'll nick
its greedies in time, strafe my mouth,
take a summer pump and cool off . . .
Dickey's what a tear in the eye'll reflect.

The more I fast the feastier he'll sing:
"I'm your medicine; your protein;
your hydro car boat; nitroglycerine
triglycerides; seasoned, appeasing

addictive. Addicts get invited, so leave
holes for roughage in your cells, or else
there'll be no room for dessert. Lose
less, multi-mineral. It's your serve."

I was twin pencils. A fit in one sex.
Began half a sketch; half, thrown dice.
Out of Mom's armoire spilled my voice;
from Dad's tux, my polka-dot socks.

Growing up man-made made me mad.
I'm dandled by a teeter totter—
no fulcrum; a hammer-haft dare.
If in me's a war, am I a war world?

Up went an end, another came down.
Where others played grace, I saw oafs
loafing on glittering snow-loaves.
Down went the other end; up came

a splintered-off, iced-on prattler,
tied in bindweed twice my size.
If pine's all that's left, set it ablaze.
No chance this fever'd get better

when trees kept saying it's summer
in winter. Maybe it isn't. Anyone
ever scribbled so off a pencil's plan
to erase its creation? No, but not never.

I'm speaking with my mother's voice
because she always told me what to say.
Because he always told me what to say,
I'm speaking with my father's voice.

Once, there was a son and a father.
The son beamed if Father got daddish.
Grounded, Dad was a dry-docked fish
off his kilter; air, his executioner.

Twice, and toothsome, the mother
esteemed so much, starlight got lost.
Steam her from inside her cedar chest
where hearts unlock boxes and wonder

beats. Up close, Dad smelled priceless,
gripping a great sea bass through the gills.
Mom softened ills with menthol apples.
To stand her, I withstood her caresses.

They're co-stars staring from my talkies,
voice-overs, visors. Their soundtracks
liven up my SWAT and splatter-flicks,
because they told me what to say, always.

Dad. He plays dead, and his leash
depreciates its lash. What's he after ·
in the afterlife? The more I dog-ear
the moors, more I sniff his ash. Hellish.

But reapers come and go, that's life,
some in rabbit ears. Remember them?
A few dogs are gentlemen. Not him.
Found him nosing the TV into my bath,

nailed him puddling inside my radio.
Snoopy. Biplane pilot. Flap-hatted
grin, sort of. Tried learning to lip-read,
you know, to talk the trash dogs do.

He keeps me awake in my sleep.
Twenty-four-seven I hear him snarl.
Caught him crouched under the table
begging for another airdropped scrap.

Should I take him out more often?
A pillow's no place to earn his wings.
This is so him: couch-hound snortings
all through Apollo's first touchdown!

Okay, here's what we did. Dad was a quark.
I took my shogun out. And the jerk grinned!
Toads marched him to where the marshland
meanders, where woods gave such a bark

I still get a wince. Open fire, said Dickey.
We loaded him, black hole, in the swamp van.
It was premium cable! I aimed at his mid-line,
silver blanked into him. He'd been less empty,

I'd have hit a vital. Roses twined in a scythe,
me and Dickey grieved. "Thou Shalt Not"
and all that smearwort. On the hospice lot,
weeds sprouted tips, like: *get a life, take a life.*

We ditched the van at first intermission,
D. and me, we'd had our glister of venom.
There once was a time I'd have said scram.
This time a guilty son gilded his stun gun.

"Hey you, what'd you do with your Dad?"
yelled the groundskeeper mowing—yawn,
at least I'm a living—hospitable grass. Then:
"can't dig here with that hole in your head."

Sieg Heil, Father, for the dammerang
Hitler lugared out of his head. Blade
pulled clean from a newborn babe,
you sang, brooded; brooded and sang.

Your long knives stole into my game
of Pimples & Indians. Skinned knees.
Your Boers warred with my Aborigines.
(Listen to me: giving a dictator dictation.)

Shepherd of Krauts, Retriever of Geld,
Farther, Fürher: ja, I heeled you, royally.
I was your hindquarters; you the Seeing Eye.
I deployed my toys in your blindside.

The Pullman pulls still. Glass cracks
a temple-level, spider web of splits.
"There you go pimping again," spits
Dickey. "He's in a safety deposit box.

We caught the stormpatriot's bluffing.
Corporeal miserable. Discharged seaman.
Those tin drums he threw? A lot of steam.
Let Baby Corporal go back to painting."

Dickey said it's the "perineum"
I dreamed. Not a blade, a spiral
licking gristle off Mom's muscle.
The loins she bore a lion from

(grave-avid at the starting gate)
parted, then departed. Inch-ward
back toward prepartum, a head
with its skull scudding after it,

lean bone: that would be me.
Me: playing skins in the infield.
Shins shining. Shit undefiled.
Me: my one and only goalie

displayed on a butcher block—
enough to make the simplest
blood-simple whimper. A beast
after birth looks like the reek

of steak. "Hey Me, Moron,"
Dickey sweets, "for the stench,
My Majesty, order a staunch.
It's *your* Peaceable Kingdom."

Mother said you count your friends on one hand.
Dickey says there are ten people for each person.
It's times like these his body adds up to mine—
it shakes mending a net or shelling an almond.

Who happens if one person becomes ten people?
They've bred like fruit flies? I'm not afraid of them.
Unless I swallow them in my sleep. Actually, I am.
I hate math; don't care how many moths flit in a bottle.

Some table wines are fine. A soldier somebody pays
tallies my fines, quarters me in his cold shoulder.
That's why I stockpile coinages: to spy a tower
of secrets, spend them, then my eyes can close.

Pennies aren't worth much, but aren't worthless.
How many an hour, minimum wage, coin of the realm—
search me, Dickey says. One arm swings, a pendulum;
the other one withers, a knobby root of cypress.

I'd knuckle down, but come on. Handshakes
with unfriendlies feel as safe as jungle gyms
monkeyed with. Take the bleachers, all thumbs.
I'll be talking to my fists. They are coiled snakes.

Black cats ring bells. I'm your son
hearing them. Cats, black or not,
are busy being cats, don't sweat it.
It's not about learning how to spin.

A whirlpool through and through, ·
you'd give geese goose bumps, get it?
No, you don't get it. Never got it.
There you sit there, you being you

not one bitter more that you used
to get used to getting used. I tried!
If only when I reached, you could.
Ouch inside a touch, you refused

fusing. I was refuse. He rode me,
but you sold me one cold wine.
Life vest hurricane weathervane.
That's all I want to say. Don't say

the drinks weren't drunk, Mother.
Yeah, he was wry enough in his gin,
liquor brokered old man, the twin
you swam with, woman. So there.

From the time he opened his mouth his talk was off.
Tuesday's today; yesterday, Sunday; Tuesday
we see Gramma Ray on Tuesday. She told a story
about the navy dockship, drunken, you dove off of.

In a tiresome sort of way it took him many times
to get to the point. Always your mitt, your tepee,
nothing on TV clicking between you and me.
I only swiped single fingers of your Seagrams.

He swears too much, but he's also excessively polite.
When man-kins got to bawling in our bodies,
I vetoed your hammering, bad company sighs.
Held them to my mirror. That's one way to edit

the nettlings out of your net, old man, no?
No, he isn't shy, and brought friends to the house
after school, took down their names and addresses.
Yes, if I said grace, I'd feel a minnow miaow

wannasays from my teeth. What's that mean?
Double-dare, dare-devil, don't go there, triple-
faced Sir. . . . Da. . . . Father, call me independable.
I won't be spoken to in scalpels.

Your yellow sun.

Mom and Dad made livings in Eden.
Mom washed water. White of Dad's eye
turned the clouds whiter. Their baby I
brought up was a melon fat as its twin.

Then God's rules poured down a storm,
drowned the infant mouth of paradise.
(It's Venus who created rain, of course,
and invented a river way out of harm . . .)

Baby seeded weeds. The farm outgrew
artichokes, clover liquor, limes, corn cribs,
plantain peels, Quakers, ostriches, crabs
in blood gravy. The irrigation ditch flew

over with fluency. From many words,
too many. Like in the Bible, the boy
in the baby made olives from honey
make money. Cuttings on sideboards,

still life with disintegrated pomegranate.
Don't blame him a thorn's in his mitten.
Or, blame him, Mom, Dad. Not one
of your entrees opened up to an exit.

Parents are the nations that thrust you
half 'n half into The Quiz. That's what
parents engineer, and you jump into it.
Vegetable manuals; rooks, ruts; and so

when somebody asks me my name,
I'll think twice, since I was given it
away and, in my opinion, that's what
made mine swim, but yeah, it's Tim

at times. Their ploys were Bull and Woo.
Taught me to pronounce a winter wren
trill like a house wren. I'd already flown
from home, and didn't they even know?

I knew: people in trios don't survive.
Now I'm a curious binocular, floored by
the ocean flowering two dives a day.
And fish are flying like petals are alive!

It's the beginning of believing season.
Time to keep an eye on me, a right eye
up-brought to mind my left-behind I—
since it's less than seconds till I'm born.

Dickey's death feels all over me.
I try not digging at the thing. He died
before I could grow his hemlock seed.
Boyo, the tricksters of this cemetery,

long-sleeved shorts with their shirts off,
can't tell a cow's dead till it's slaughtered.
He was a sublime Halloween snicker,
bat dark meat. Never watched golf.

Not much now but gum and minerals,
blue pods, tainted entertainments.
Our folder warps, drifts, frags, taunts.
Everest ground down to soil samples.

I've lost my sprite, my shot at distemper,
nobody's rabies can pillow this blow.
Nobody's but Dickey's. My "he" is "O,"
who once flicked hearts, a lamplighter.

I could clang wish-bells, break out a dish,
but I know he's the headache at the base
of my throat. He's left ice in my voice,
foam round rocks where we used to fish.

"He's gone," Mother Teresa told me.
"Let him. Had to hit delete sometime.
When your grief's over, give the lame
neckties. It's starfish we pity." Really,

he was piano, and pianos never mind
whose key gets dumbed down. Playing,
he had an unlabored way of weaseling
out of bedtime: theorize the never-land

of time. Smart-ass. Dry ice. Head shot.
I found him chewed through by mice.
Funeral Fugue on Triangle, of course.
Bedside Terry, grace on her, got a sheet

and despite my assonating roar,
my nutso speech about chicken soup—
flaxed his face. Well, brought-up
golden as he'd been, locks of hair

raced his last track. Done. Dear Ms. T.,
suture my en- to my em-dashes; please
imprint this apostrophe: "Prince I miss,
I'd lay lions to spring you back, my boy."

First I denied the no-seeums speckling
my dead boy. *Over here*, they called.
I overheard *there*. My shoulder thawed,
felt fine. I exhaled my unson's song.

Then came blame. Used up, I sued it.
Anger management? I nail-gunned
flies all over drywall. My tantrum
plucked a geshrunken dish; threw it, it

pitched back, *thew!* Pawed hardball,
return me his birthdays. I'll be prompt
to Commencement, promise. I'm unkempt?
I'll kempt. But worms don't dicker a deal . . .

I resigned my shift; I mean, took a break.
Blanket our dog wouldn't even adopt,
I laid off apostrophes to the teardrop.
His name sank, forsook all heartache—

no more pantomime palominos.
If you can't stage miracles, curtain.
It's not like you become Adam, even
whistling to the herd in widow grass.

If the raw world left in me is red,
how do I get from here to the rest
of the world? Wasp in my nest
with software forepaws, D's dead

body bugs me for an asbestos
uniform. Would have bled, allowed.
Wanted to swap tongues for broad
swords. Finger-happy to his toes'

Keds, over he went: land mines,
fortress railings sharpening spears.
Family plots ought to enlist snipers.
I'll say. I'll spit, stick to my guns.

How will I howl by myself outside,
little egger, without reinforcements?—
well, we'll see then, won't we. Laments
need seeds. Back when he got all dyed,

I didn't want me going red and didn't.
Blood on the curbside, my man of war,
heal, he told me, *you can't seal a scar
without a fight or weapons to win it.*

I hear, in my phone, vocabulary where
he's not there, and head for a textbook.
Unless I leave him be I'll get a smack.
I leaf through movies, see smoke and fire,

race round in rings, get woozy and fall
asleep, dream up an exit. You would too.
A burned man gripped straw. People do,
you know: water their palms. Big deal.

What if your brother was a child of five
and cried the eyes nighthawks hunt with?
Once a babe in khaki shorts gave birth
to ashes in a lobby. Who would you save,

stuck on a horse, your recourse a pony
to the circus? Bottom-feeders suck it to go,
till their guts sag. "How was the show?"
asked a toucan. What would you say?

Dear ears, his eyes kept peered for you.
There was stereo, no paring needed.
He seemed so healthy, witty, so glad
with all the tripwires we'd run through.

Dear eyes, my ears kept paired for you,
no stereo's here. No peelings heeded.
You look unhealthy like that: scalloped.
With all the duophrenia you listen to,

it was boded we'd run out of each other.
Look. Talk's short. I'll always worry
when I don't hear the sled of causality
in the fog, or the otherness in another

sounds like there's nobody there
on the bus. Hard to hear like myself
in that atmosphere, bag of mouth,
table talk between salt and pepper.

But look at them. Grandparent-solid.
Turrets you could use as chess-pieces.
Makes you go retro for a family tree's
entreaty. If a seed, I know, is behelded,

it plants in us a pretty heady casualty.
No need to answer; really, no need.
What would I do if you did? I did
keep you in mind, brother, didn't he?

A finch in my chest flinches to get
heard. Wingman sewed it in. I hear
the *chi-chuwee chuwee* achew in there,
tiny beck beating the big heartbeat.

Mind you, it takes brains to slice
open a hide, scoop out the marble
muscles; craze a rib cage; uncoil
the aorta; slide in a gift like his:

the elf chirruping in my self, itself
elfin (the self's wit-part part want).
Pity I'm not someone else's heart!—
elf elsewhere, another body's grief.

I don't mind my beater's a warbler,
or how in-the-skin is the finch's cry.
Eat sweat, wet seat: its homunculi
pinions ping in my rock tumbler's

cavity. I place my ear to my chest.
Finch-flitters from the solar-plexus,
beaky reminders keep keeping pace.
Oh my minute pecks, tend your nest.

Iris of the one-eyed Satan—see it?
X-ray of a horse pout about to eat me.
Amputee kissing a double amputee.
Exploded nova; no, what an idiot

I am: fly gotten crushed by a shovel.
That black is somebody's childhood
shit spread on a microscope slide.
(If *e* cuts in line, evil becomes vile.)

A woman's shadow on her back, legs
open, like pudding's been splattened
by a bullet-train's million-mile second.
Take away the veins, that's the bags

I stuffed my faces in before their faces
mixed each other up and made mine.
What a kid drew in Art Class, a brain-
dead kid. Not sure what that clot is—

or they're smudges, maybe inkblots?
Somebody dripped ink on paper, folded
the paper top to bottom or side to side.
The ink blotted and created inkblots.

I shake my head, my right brain's
left behind; my left, right behind.
I mean, I'll tell you what I found
so fine about flushing my coins

down a well. Splashes answered.
I marbled the moon with a wand.
Boy o boy, hello shook my hand,
the water's underworld stirred

to a tune of midnight, midnight.
I didn't much mind how timepieces
cramped my moon-in-man aphasias.
But I wouldn't—I *won't*—let daylight

phase me out. Weighed too well,
gelatin glummed in my mouth,
I tasted gypsum. Smack! Health
care rusted the fly in my flywheel.

Realignment? Right, two planets
balled up into one hard-boiled sun.
You double helical worms, I've won,
stares back-spinning out my orbits.

Back on my wings, wings became me.
I banked, broke, beside myself. Besides,
honeysuckle sang, and riverwards
ran the overrun beds of brooks, see?—

but no meadow. Never was a meadow.
Lots of long division, and times tables
where once there were standing pools.
If you played into them you got polio.

Polished glass wading downstream,
oaks barked their spells, and hex-books
cracked, spine-open. Those are *facts*.
None of that sailor-ruby-sky eventime.

Red robin, red robin, bash again, again
against my window, feathers in flame
—a fireman's?—to get in. Or be calm
to the lunatic squires in your bloodline.

Your beak-and-pockings won't open
more living room. You're so enamored
of mates you don't know your mirrored
yew from yew. So bloody your reflection.

Don't have to swim straight, dark says.
Two rhymes snagged between rhymes,
spun puns, all my blinds up in flames.
The voices in noise are getting wise:

make peace with thunder's lightning—
ozone scent, ball-peen, fork in a path.
A bit more person, less son underneath:
proven, so what's with the worrying

spinning the hub of your compass?
At broken levees, the outcast is recast
with dirt's permanent dirt, and a coast.
A spinnaker, spoiled, still sails at ease.

Stand on banks of the standard god.
Why he's hiding from me's beyond me.
Spider lilies reach out. One artery's
blood-flow is affluent enough fluid.

What do people believe in? If adrift,
twirl a world, find a loco-habitation—
not exactly continent, inexactly home.
With so much left, no wonder I'm aloft.

So I left my apartment, got down where
I tried getting going outgoing. You know,
taking control, like when you say "hello
there, Blue Beautiful." Bossed me over

to the bar to make noise out of nonsense.
Why do people wear hair? Because it spirals?
Why does my stucco computer store girls
who say o jeez not him? Frankensense,

my eyes bled resin, hardened to tears.
Out of her rocks, or at least rocky soil,
I wanted the class of her bloom; smell,
aroma. How her was mine; mine, hers?

Since you asked, please remember: not
answering is no odder than Nevada's
name. Nevada, my muskalot sonata's
non grata. Called her after her street.

Goodnight kisses, traded in ice trays.
What's in a touch? A zillion electrons
repulsed by somebody's other zillions.
Lay down light, dear gone-as-always.

Damned if my thumbs-up, deadpan
candyman didn't send me a fairy!
Named her Serena, or maybe Holly.
We crept clear of those holy chosen

on the rubber of schoolyard trickeries.
A blacktop dripped syrup on a roll.
Rumors, at recess, twirled in snowfall,
made swings hurl, bloody bent knees.

The bullies shot tanks, I'll give you that.
Except for raptors, storybook pigs, ducks
after dark, archangels wielding axes,
I didn't much worry for the most part—

but Christmas, Holly died. Weird.
Hail of rainstones against her window.
"You saw that," Serena said, "didn't you?"
What furies I saw the weather pulled

wool over. Want more from my story?—
I hear your neck, cricketing as you nod.
I've owed Serena letters, worded in red,
since elementary. Maybe I'll marry Holly.

When I saw her, her face was a marinade
in bleach, her face was a marinade in bleach
when I didn't. Women don't need much
installation. They come 99 percent installed.

Before we plugged in and went stringy,
we sucked fingers, armed to the bone. Teeth,
napes, and legs laid into each other's length.
Horn through the hole: horn A, hole B.

Belly up, bedroom behind our backs, what
better bite of a stick stuck between our lips
than one face shadowing another's eclipse?
A skim of breath, a word from her heat

and I went chuck, and chewed my elbows.
Too many thrills, too much soul dissolves.
The more your tongue slips, the less it solves.
Don't say you never greased *your* jowls.

Alright, she also wrote all over my face:
wrong, wrong. (What I meant to vent's getting
twisted up.) She hooked me under her wing
all right. No good comes of goddesslessness.

I moved inside a movie about women
who milked men. Man, one murmur
could've wormed venom out of a tiger
snake. Manhandled all of Manhattan.

Seraph cigarette. Flicked. Sipped. I
hightailed ten tanned slicks into a bar,
lobbied till I needed to tip the tender
to watch. Pollen thickened into honey.

Yeah I keep a watch. Used to wear clocks
out in a day. Benders at The Firethrower,
yessir, bent her, framed her eyesore; or . . .
Bellboys played boys' bells and desk clerks

desk clerks. That's how yesterlate air raid
sirens lured men to The Island, bad deeds
in Times Square sweetened to sweat beads.
Some men can barely say "masquerade"

and their silver unreels. Really, that's all
we running men run after. The money shot.
The bed seeded; done, the rampant feat,
we limp up to cradle, sad, in a drizzle.

Noise-canceling paws at my ears
blacked out their hackwork back
talk. See how clear I hear? Think
no rustle-in-the-reeds-clear, dears.

Verbalburnalizations left blisters.
No high fives for me. A low whir
collared around the water cooler.
Suited in leagues, the winners

aced their crook tests into college,
majored in Collage or File in Blank,
kick-started resumes. Invisible ink,
I flunked Medley; in Hodgepodge

took a pass. Pardon my self-pity.
The sky cries liberal when it rains.
It's the Aspie in me. Dissociation's
affidavits. I had a couple buddies—

only, no; no friends. Just because
these paws paused wilderness howls,
I'd have gladly tuned in anyone else's
self-pity parties. Or just because . . .

. . . nobody's safe inside the airtight zones
the saved fly blind in, and they aren't saved.
People drive deaf and dumb, because jade
rain's always blazing out their cell phones.

I'm not scared of enemies, just their velocity.
When a starling comes out, it's an incisor,
a scissor of ire, key swallowed, a seedy stare.
When stares start, there's no stopping the eye.

People are in pain inside their membranes.
A blue forehead vine earmarks those people
to other people whose skin is made of marble.
People whisper to brushing people in trains:

super lunar windows, loops, straps, rings.
I hang onto those things if I ride the subways.
Otherwise, pickpockets get pecs in my eyes.
I can't pick the pettings from the walletings.

I hate how faces rhyme for days at a time,
then they *seem* seen, then they look at you,
then stop looking like faces. I saw that blue
vine in me too. Scissored it out, vein by vein.

The Trimínos rent free in my head.
They can get wiry, but that's fine,
long as their tarnations don't turn on.
They drive the Duelatives inside

out. Those scum in my soulway
gummed up the bath roots in soil.
Bad timing, fly puke on his lapel,
I was *fucked*. Dad bootstrapped me

then varmint-rifled Mom, twice
times nine times. His gun sprang,
barreled back, double boomerang.
I let my monoxide sucking apparatus

set off every alarm in the house—
not enough—brainstormed a flight
plan, but adios couldn't reckon it.
Now that I'm leased to my Trimínos,

the Duelatives defuel their feuding—
no more roaming, gloamy, at home.
What's a Trimíno? In the mudroom
hang three hats, where no hats hung.

In your sleep they rant what's left of you.
Others bring blockheadedness. Their voices chime
brainswoons. Snow carpets alyssum by the asylum.
They're jumbo, you know, not mumbo,

feral sheikhs, in the sheets, amigo.
Wrecked rexes, they preach shrieks,
refluxes inbred, steppe-tundra freeze reflex.
A good sniff, out snorts an inner wooly rhino.

Catnapping synapses need grease.
Otherwise, a fusty, erstwhile rapscallion,
runner-up misnomer, antidisestablishmentarianism.
Not much fruit in siestas shallow as a crease.

When your reverie is to cop
to Dr. Hopeful (and he's fond of you, fearfully,
but talks like a prep), they'll perp up like Psyche.
Their tongues exceed mouthings, their viles go deep.

Think this dream through—
you're a souvenir? witchcrafter from Salem?
horse-drawn monarch, comeliest in your kingdom?
Like forty winking thieves, devils, they bedevil you.

You say I'm in one of my highs.
Maybe I am, and maybe my eye-
sight's an MRI, and I'm its fiancé.
I say you're in one of my belows,

so hands off my lobes, Dr. Will
Bill Ignoble. You don't have a clue.
Do I hear voices? Sure, that's you,
Administer of Miniscule Cubicles.

No way my cubicle's miniscule—
people talk to me in tinny hoards
eddying in the air, where words
herd, then hide out in a shell

shaped like an ear, like Africa's
shaped like an elephant's ear.
My mind thinks like an islander.
You rave to me about manias

as if D's still here. Miss him.
Mr. Headphone's been on the fritz
since ages ago we itched itches.
Miss him miss him miss him.

Your head meds serve my serfdom.
Pile on, pill after pill. Chemistry's
dixie cap of curt, dried, swilled peas.
My greyhound runs aground, dumb

bunny. I'm itching poppies in my ears.
Dig too deep, I'll scratch my tympanum
(been meaning anyway to anvil the villain).
Coated shark teeth, like pinking shears,

cut zigzags out of my cerebrum's zing.
Enchanting chants on vellum?—gone.
The reptile?—wrapped in mammal skin.
What's *with* me? I was born whizzing,

then you guys poked dents in my Pills-
bury badboy, a new *don't* every minute.
Mood, mood, nod away; loosen my knot,
not me, you twitch. Here comes Haldol's

hiccups. Go easy, guys, on Puke Center,
okay? Guys! Guys? Guys. Dopeheads.
Snoozed (*otherwise cause nausea*), I'm eased
into my cell, and O, man. Is. This. Blear.

Words next-to-last-next-to-last-next-to
smoke haze, a granite edge, and no ledge
I know of. When I'm in a thought-plunge,
never can trust what I feel I think I know.

And so I'm down over, of all words,
those that buzz like . . . like . . . I don't
grasp them. Flies, I mean. But the stunt,
done right, is something: fist the bastards.

End of scrutiny; of subject to rethinking;
of mortification (if you're not wrong, me);
of one last thing I need to say to you: sorry
won't unprison a bit. Not that I'm angling

for time done, or yakking for forgiveness.
I see I didn't have to hurt me, not a finger
needled. Swat furies and they fly stronger.
Who'd do the damned penance in my place?

I spent a whole day working on my spin.
Thinking is the key, keeps catching its latch.
We can't start even close to from scratch . . .
scratch that. I'm too red even to start from.

Dickey my door, I'm seeing. Yesterday
I can tackle after all, and I feel like it
opens an ocean view from my parapet
of mountains and moons of Mercury.

Beaches needed badges on Neptune,
remember? To give us a memory,
Pisces, I christened you Gemini.
Nebula. Ash. Steam from a Dune.

We pitched tents in contentments.
We sanded castles. Me? Your factory
of Radioplasma. You, my stationery
output, now stay put. No complaints.

Dr. Rivers sees to it my seas belong.
His orderlies tip white-caps at me
like I'm a stranded merman. Dickey,
my buoyed-up somebody, unsung

island gone inland, you swam out
of my blues, but our duo disordered
the herds. Nobody played shepherd.
Well now, you and I are words apart.

I feel well, but keep hoping to get well—
not just better, you know. But every day
I get well, I hope on the following day
I'll feel better, but instead I feel . . . Well

At times I feel so much, I think
I'm sentimental. Come to think of it,
maybe it's just thought, and I feel

nothing much at all. We live
one life living, another thinking.
Which one's true, which false?

The worst fate: to spend a life
thinking, until that life is not
the life you felt you lived.

—after Pessoa

NOTES

"A page writes me" is loosely based on an example in Eugen Bleuler's 1911 study, *Dementia Praecox or the Group of Schizophrenias* (International Universities Press, 1950), p. 17.

Lines 17–18 in "I was twin pencils"; lines 1–3 in "I hear, in my phone, vocabulary where"; and the neologism "crusady" in "My tongue print's on your butter" derive from *Disordered Thinking and Schizophrenic Psychopathology*, by Martin Harrow and Donald M. Quinlan (Gardner Press, 1985), pp. 422, 426, and 427.

"My notion of heaven" adapts some diction from an example in "A Receptive Language Deficit in Schizophrenic Thought Disorder," by Keith R. Laws, Tejinder K. Kondel, and Peter J. McKenna, *Cognitive Neuropsychiatry*, 4 (2), p. 95.

The scenario and last line in "Okay, here's what what we did. Dad was a quark" derive from an example of delusional confabulation in *Schizophrenia and Related Syndromes*, Second Edition, by P.J. McKenna (Routledge, 2007), pp. 5–6.

"From the time he opened his mouth he talk was off" adapts some phrasing from *Autism: Explaining the Enigma*, by Uta Frith (Wiley Blackwell, 2003), p. 3.

"In your sleep they rant what's left of you" adapts some diction from an example in Emil Kraepelin's 1913 study, *Dementia Praecox and Paraphrenia* (Robert E. Krieger Publishing Company, Inc., 1971), p. 194.

The *cufflinks / handcuffs* pun in "I feel as male as I feel female" derives from an example in *Schizophrenic Speech: Making Sense of Bathroots and Ponds that Fall in*

Doorways, by Peter J, McKenna and Tomasina Oh (Cambridge University Press, 2005), p. 115.

The *hydro-car-boat* pun in "I cut back on coffee. And air. And sky" derives from "The Significance of Thought Disorder in Diagnostic Evaluations," by N. J. C. Andreasen, Ming T. Tsuang, and Arthur Canter, *Comprehensive Psychiatry,* (1974), 15, p. 29.

Anna Asquith

STEVEN CRAMER is the author of four previous poetry collections: *The Eye that Desires to Look Upward* (1987), *The World Book* (1992), *Dialogue for the Left and Right Hand* (1997), and *Goodbye to the Orchard* (Sarabande, 2004), which won the 2005 Sheila Motton Prize from the New England Poetry Club and was named a 2005 Honor Book in Poetry by the Massachusetts Center for the Book. His poems and reviews have appeared in numerous literary journals, including *AGNI, Antioch Review, The Atlantic Monthly, Field, Kenyon Review, The Nation, The New England Review, The New Republic, The Paris Review, Partisan Review, Ploughshares, Poetry, Slate,* and *Triquarterly.* His work has been represented in anthologies such as *The Autumn House Anthology of Contemporary American Poetry, Villanelles,* and *The POETRY Anthology, 1912–2002.* He has also written chapters for *Simply Lasting: Writers on Jane Kenyon; Touchstones: American Poets on a Favorite Poem;* and *Until Everything Is Continuous Again: American Poets on the Recent Work of W. S. Merwin.* Recipient of fellowships from the Massachusetts Artists Foundation and the National Endowment for the Arts, he has taught literature and writing at Bennington College, Boston University, M.I.T., and Tufts University. He currently directs the Low-Residency MFA Program in Creative Writing at Lesley University, in Cambridge.

Sarabande Books thanks you for the purchase of this book; we do hope you enjoy it! Founded in 1994 as an independent, nonprofit, literary press, Sarabande publishes poetry, short fiction, and literary nonfiction—genres increasingly neglected by commercial publishers. We are committed to producing beautiful, lasting editions that honor exceptional writing, and to keeping those books in print. If you're interested in further reading, take a moment to browse our website, www.sarabandebooks.org. There you'll find information about other titles; opportunities to contribute to the Sarabande mission; and an abundance of supporting materials including audio, video, a lively blog, and our Sarabande in Education program.